ANIMAL MIGRATION

Malcolm Penny

Illustrated by Vanda Baginska

The Bookwright Press
New York · 1987

The Animal Kingdom

Animal Evolution
Animal Homes
Animal Migration
Animals and their Young

First published in the
United States in 1987 by
The Bookwright Press
387 Park Avenue South
New York, NY 10016

First published in 1987 by
Wayland (Publishers) Ltd
61 Western Road, Hove
East Sussex BN3 1JD, England

ISBN 0–531–18123–5

Library of Congress Catalog Card Number: 87–70387

Typeset by DP Press, Sevenoaks, Kent, England
Printed by Casterman SA, Belgium

Contents

The reasons for migration

Migration is the name given to regular movements of whole populations of animals from one place to another and back again, as conditions change. In the tropics, animals move in response to the dry season and rainy season. In the sea, small animals in the plankton migrate every day. As the sun rises, they sink deeper in the water because the sunlight is too bright for them. Later, as the daylight fades, they drift toward the surface again.

The most common form of migration, carried out by millions of animals every year, is into colder areas during the summer, and back to warmer parts of the world for the winter. Geese, for example, leave temperate countries in spring to fly north to the Arctic, often across stormy seas. Why do they take the risk? Like many birds, they go north to breed.

The map below shows the migration routes of some well known migrants.

During the short Arctic summer, geese find plenty of food for their young because few other animals live there all year round. Also there is less danger from predators than there is in their winter homes. This is important for the adults as well, because they become unable to fly every summer, when they molt to grow new feathers.

Humans migrate, too. Nomadic tribes, such as the Bedouin, spend the dry season near oases in the Arabian desert. In the rainy season they wander with their sheep and camels to find new grass for the animals. In northern Scandinavia, the Lapps follow their herds of reindeer north in summer and south again in winter.

All kinds of animals migrate – insects and birds fly thousands of miles over land and sea, whales and fish swim around the vast oceans, while herds of animals trek across the land. In this book we shall look at some of their amazing journeys.

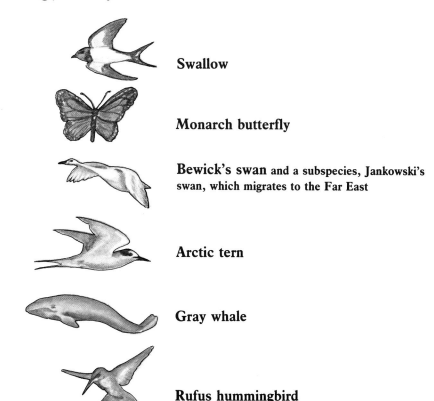

Swallow

Monarch butterfly

Bewick's swan and a subspecies, Jankowski's swan, which migrates to the Far East

Arctic tern

Gray whale

Rufus hummingbird

Timing the move

All over the world, people notice the migration of animals, especially birds, and recognize them as signs of the changing seasons. Usually, the animals get it right: for example, as summer begins in the Northern Hemisphere, swallows fly from South Africa to Europe. Similarly, after spending the summer around the Arctic in order to breed, geese fly south to spend the winter in warmer areas. To time their movements so accurately, the birds must be alert to changes in their surroundings that may be too small for humans to notice.

Whatever the weather, the one thing that does not change in a particular place at a particular date is the length of time between sunrise and sunset. This is known as the "daylength." Almost every living thing is affected by daylength. This means plants as well as animals.

Daylength affects birds by making them restless when the days are getting longer in spring, or shorter in autumn. Nobody is really sure how it works, but they seem to become more sensitive to changes in the atmosphere at these times. As winter changes to spring, the air becomes warmer and the wind changes direction. Most of these changes are so gradual that humans do not notice them until after they have happened. The birds, however, are already on the move.

A European flower called the greater celandine, or swallow flower, opens at the same time as the swallows arrive. This is because the flower is responding to the same changes in daylength and temperature as the birds.

Opposite *Canada geese arrive at their wintering ground in the United States.*

Finding the way

When animals make long journeys across places where there is no food or shelter, such as deserts or oceans, it is very important that they should be able to navigate accurately.

Birds find their way by the stars at night, and by the sun during the day. People thought that this was impossible until some migrating birds were put in cages inside a planetarium. When the operator turned the artificial sky around, the birds gathered at the sides of the cages nearest to the direction in which they would have flown if the sky had been real. Every time he moved it, the birds moved to a new position. This proved that they could see the stars and respond to them.

Snow geese and sandhill cranes arrive in Bosque del Apache wildlife reserve in New Mexico to spend the winter.

However, a navigator must have an accurate clock, because the stars seem to move as the earth rotates.

Many animals, especially birds, have a very precise sense of time, which is called their "internal clock." In cloudy weather, birds delay setting off on long journeys, but if the cloud lasts for a long time, they must eventually go, to complete their migration in time. In such conditions, they are able to steer by following the magnetic field of the earth. We could say that they have their own special compasses inside them, which tell them the right direction.

Most migrating animals travel in groups, sometimes in very large numbers. This makes it more likely that they will find the right way, especially when the group includes experienced animals that have made the journey before.

Thrushes and robins navigate by the stars. Pictured below are the European robin and song thrush.

The diagram below shows how a bird in a planetarium follows the stars, as the artificial sky is moved around.

Swallows and banding

People wondered for centuries where swallows went in the winter, when they disappeared from Europe. Some scientists believed that they hibernated!

Now their movements are quite well known because some birds have been marked with lightweight metal leg bands, each stamped with a number. When a bird is caught again, or found dead, it is possible to find out when and where the band was first put on.

The results show that before winter arrives, European swallows leave Europe and fly to South Africa, where it is summer. This is because South Africa lies in the Southern Hemisphere, which has summer when the Northern Hemisphere has winter. When spring returns in the Northern Hemisphere, they move northward across Africa and the Mediterranean with the flow of warm air. The same species in North America, where it is called the barn swallow, avoids the northern winter by flying to South America, where it is summer.

Because the change of the seasons occurs at a slightly different time each year, the swallows return to the North on different dates. However, they arrive within the same two week period every year, in the second half of April. A pair of swallows uses the same nest site year after year.

There is a saying, "one swallow doesn't make a summer." This means that one or two birds often arrive before the main flocks, only to be caught by a late frost. Summer has truly begun only when the large flocks arrive.

Opposite *A flock of swallows arrive in late April to breed in Europe. The yellow flowers of greater celandine are already open.*

Below *The painted lady of Europe and the U.S. and the clouded yellow of Africa and Europe.*

Below *The painted lady of Europe and the U.S. and the clouded yellow of Africa and Europe.*

The map below shows the various migration routes of the monarch butterfly.

Migrating butterflies

The monarch, or milkweed butterfly, is well known for its amazing migration. In the town of Pacific Grove in California, people hold a street festival every winter, when the monarchs return from across the Canadian border in the north.

On the eastern side of Canada, the monarch butterflies set out on a much longer migration. Monarchs, which breed as far north as Quebec, fly 3,000 km (1,860 mi) south to Mexico. When they arrive there in October, they roost in huge swarms in the mountain forests, where they spend the winter.

At the beginning of March, they start to migrate north once more, flying at about 18 km (11 mi) an hour. As they travel, the females pause to lay eggs on milkweed plants. When the eggs hatch, and after the caterpillars have pupated, the newly emerged adults continue the journey north.

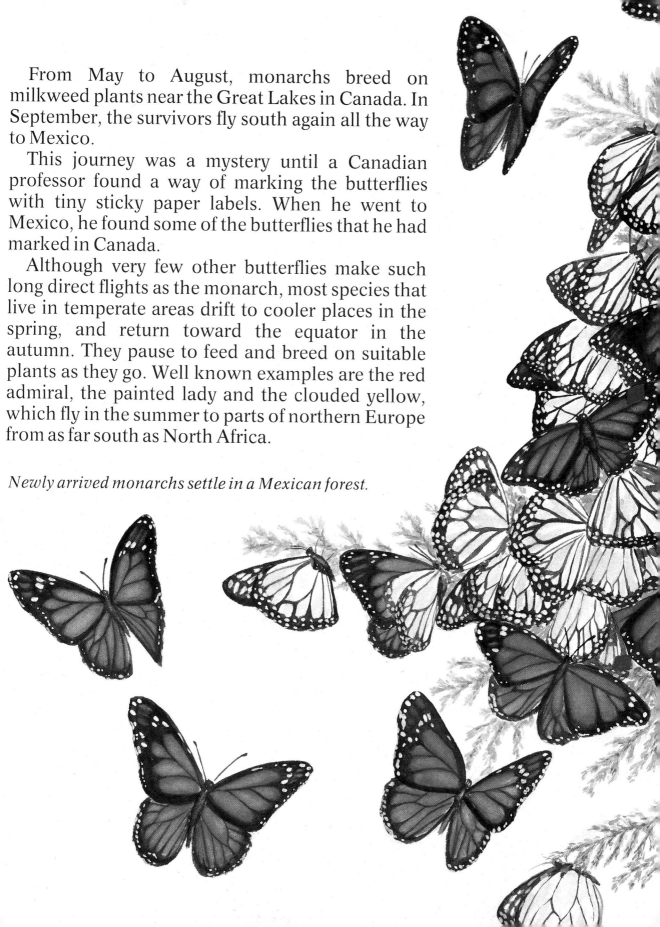

From May to August, monarchs breed on milkweed plants near the Great Lakes in Canada. In September, the survivors fly south again all the way to Mexico.

This journey was a mystery until a Canadian professor found a way of marking the butterflies with tiny sticky paper labels. When he went to Mexico, he found some of the butterflies that he had marked in Canada.

Although very few other butterflies make such long direct flights as the monarch, most species that live in temperate areas drift to cooler places in the spring, and return toward the equator in the autumn. They pause to feed and breed on suitable plants as they go. Well known examples are the red admiral, the painted lady and the clouded yellow, which fly in the summer to parts of northern Europe from as far south as North Africa.

Newly arrived monarchs settle in a Mexican forest.

Swans with names

At first sight, one swan looks much like another. If we look at them more closely, however, there is a sure way to identify individuals in one species.

The method of identifying Bewick's swans was discovered in England. Sir Peter Scott, a famous naturalist, found that he could recognize individual Bewick's swans by the patterns on their bills. He gave the birds names. From then on, it was possible to follow their family life when the swans came back from their breeding grounds in Siberia every autumn.

Now we know that the pairs stay together for life, and that they live at least twenty-five years. The parents bring the young swans with them when they leave Siberia.

A pair of Bewick's swans on a Siberian lake in summer.

The family stays together during the first winter. In February they return together to Siberia, flying across Europe. On the way, the swans meet others, which have spent the winter in Ireland, or elsewhere in Britain. They gather in favorite stopping-places, where they can rest and feed before flying on to Siberia.

As they fly from the Netherlands to West Germany and onwards across Eastern Europe, the swans become the responsibility of one country after another. The birds themselves are protected by law everywhere they go, but it is just as important to protect the estuaries and marshes that they need as resting-places on the way.

There are other swans that migrate in a similar way in North America, and they probably share a similar family life. So far, however, nobody has found out how to tell them apart like the Bewick's swans.

Herds of the frozen North

Around the Arctic Circle in Scandinavia, Siberia, Canada and Alaska live huge herds of reindeer, or caribou. They are a single species, called "caribou" in North America and "reindeer" in Europe and Asia. Around the Arctic Circle, winters are long and very cold, and summers are brief. During the winter, the deer shelter in the forests to the south of the Arctic Circle, but they migrate to the north for the summer, to graze on the tundra.

Caribou travel as much as 1,000 km (620 mi) in each direction. The females lead the way, beginning in early spring. They walk about 450 km (280 mi) until they reach one of their regular calving-grounds, where they give birth. On these wild, exposed hillsides they are safer from predators.

When the calves are born, the herd moves on. By now the males and young caribou from previous years have caught up with the main herd.

A caribou herd grazes on the tundra as snow melts in the Arctic summer. With them are two young Lapp herders wearing traditional dress.

A Lapp herder in a boat leads caribou across water to their summer pastures in the north of Norway.

The calves can run a few hours after they are born, and the herd moves quickly to the far northern pastures. There they feed on the tundra plants, such as mosses and lichens.

By September, the tundra begins to freeze again, the plants die off, and the caribou must move into the forests once more. There the deep snow is soft enough for them to find food underneath.

In Lapland, reindeer are traditionally followed by nomadic tribes called Lapps, who move with them along the migratory journey. They protect the animals from bears and wolves, and make use of their milk, skins and meat.

Herds of the African plains

The great herds of wildebeest, zebra and Thomson's gazelles that live on the African plains migrate in search of fresh grass to eat. During the dry season, they feed in open woodlands near Lake Victoria, but when the rainy season begins in December, they move out onto the open grasslands of the Serengeti plain. For the next three months they wander around the plain, always moving toward places where rain is falling, to eat the fresh, young grass. Sometimes they follow thunder clouds as much as 100 km (62 mi) away.

The grass that springs up in the rainy season lasts the herds for another three months, until the plains become too dry. In June, they migrate back to the woodlands by the lake, where the grass has recovered and there is still plenty of water.

Farther to the north, in the Sudan, another migration occurs. During the rainy season, the Nile River floods. Enormous herds of kob antelope are driven south, as the water spreads 800 km (500 mi) across the plain.

When the rains stop, the kob move slowly northward again. They follow the flooded area, feeding on the grass that grows as the land dries. As the huge herds move northward, they can find fresh grass every day. Later in the dry season, when the grass has all been eaten, the kob must move south again, to meet the approaching rains. Like wildebeest, they gallop toward every thunder cloud they can see or hear. Soon the rainy season starts, the river overflows, and the kob are driven far to the south to begin all over again.

On the Serengeti plain in Africa, herds of wildebeest follow rainclouds to find fresh grass.

The rare whooping crane

A whooping crane egg is placed in the nest of a sandhill crane in Idaho.

Every autumn, a small flock of whooping cranes arrives at Aransas, on the coast of Texas. There are only about one hundred of them left. They became so rare because the marshes where they nested were drained and made into farmland. Until 1955 their remaining breeding place was a mystery. Then it was discovered in Alberta in northwestern Canada. At that time there were only twenty-one birds alive. Since then, their numbers have increased very slowly and the birds have a safe home in Wood Buffalo National Park, Alberta.

The reason for their slow recovery is that they are very special migrants. They will nest only in the area where their parents take them on their first migratory flight, nearly 4,000 km (2,480 mi) from Canada to Texas. Although there are other suitable breeding and wintering places, the cranes will not use them.

Another unusual feature of whooping cranes is that, although they lay two eggs, one of their chicks always dies in its first two weeks of life. To increase the number of cranes, scientists took one egg from each of twelve nests in Canada, and put them in the nests of sandhill cranes, which breed in Idaho, in the United States. They hoped that each sandhill crane would look after the whooping crane chick as if it were its own.

Sandhill cranes migrate as well, but only a little over 1,000 km (620 mi), to New Mexico. When the baby whooping cranes hatched and grew up, they followed the sandhill cranes on their migration. Now there are two populations of this rare bird.

Opposite *Some whooping cranes in the marshes of Aransas, Texas. The birds arrive each autumn in order to spend the winter there.*

The migratory route of the whooping crane from to Canada Texas

Seabirds

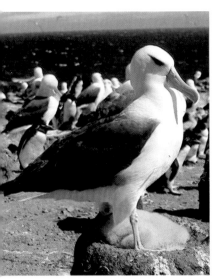

Black-browed albatrosses share their breeding ground in the Falkland Islands with rockhopper penguins.

Birds that spend most of their lives at sea must come to land in order to breed. Some of them fly great distances. Great shearwaters breed in the Falklands and other South Atlantic islands during the southern summer. In March, when their breeding season is over, they begin to move northward, up the coasts of South and North America. Then they cross the Atlantic, flying over Greenland and Iceland, and in August they are often seen near the British Isles. From there they move south once more, down the coast of Africa, reaching their breeding islands in November. They fly a journey of over 20,000 km (12,400 mi).

The short-tailed shearwater is another long-distance flier. Each autumn these birds leave their breeding ground in southeast Australia and fly to the Bering Straits off Alaska.

The champion migrant of the world is the Arctic tern. It breeds as far north as northern Greenland, but spends its non-breeding season in the Antarctic. It has two summers every year, and no winter. As it flies its annual journey of over 40,000 km (24,800 mi), it sees more daylight than any other living creature.

Not all seabird migrations are on such a vast scale. Auks, such as puffins and guillemots, leave their breeding sites in the North Atlantic, Pacific and Arctic Oceans at the end of the summer, to spend the winter on the open sea. There they are safe from the danger of being washed ashore by storms.

Puffins can only fly for short distances, but they are superb swimmers. Penguins of the Southern Hemisphere cannot fly at all, but they may swim northward when the southern winter begins.

Opposite *A flock of migrating Arctic terns.*

Migrating fish

A group of young Sargasso eels.

Salmon hatch in fresh water. Along the western seaboard of North America they usually start to migrate to the sea in their second year. In Britain they leave at about one-year-old, but in northern Canada or Norway it may take them eight years.

Salmon spend up to four years at sea. Salmon from many different rivers mingle together, but when the time comes to return to fresh water to breed, each goes to the river where it hatched, and even to the same patch of gravel. They recognize the place by its smell, which they remember from when they were babies.

Salmon from the Pacific Ocean die when they have bred once, but Atlantic salmon, especially in Canada, may survive to return to sea and breed again in the following season.

Eels live in just the opposite way. They hatch in the Sargasso Sea in the western Atlantic, and migrate to fresh water when they are old enough. There are two separate species in the Sargasso. The North American eel leaves to find fresh water when it is one-year-old, while the European eel stays at sea for three years.

Young eels are transparent. When they first swim up rivers they are called elvers. When they are six or seven years old they turn silver. Now they are ready to leave and return to the Sargasso Sea to breed.

The bluefin tuna fish, or tunnyfish, migrate great distances in search of food. Scientists have tagged them and traced their journey from the waters off Florida and the Bahamas, where they spawn in June, up to Nova Scotia, 2,500 km (1,550 mi) north.

Opposite *Two salmon leap up a waterfall as they return to their freshwater breeding ground from the sea.*

Marine mammals

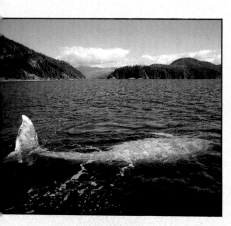

A gray whale surfaces near Vancouver Island, Canada.

Humpback whales spend the polar summer around the North or South Pole, feeding on the mass of krill in the sea. When the summer ends, however, the water soon freezes over, so the whales must leave. They migrate almost 5,000 km (3,100 mi) from the Poles to warmer tropical waters, where they breed. They return to polar waters when summer begins again. The two populations of humpback whales never meet because when one is in tropical waters avoiding a polar winter, the other is enjoying summer at the other pole.

There is only one population of gray whales. They spend the summer in the Arctic, and migrate down the west coast of the U.S. to Mexico for the winter.

There they gather in sheltered lagoons to mate and produce their calves. The round trip of about 20,000 km (12,400 mi) takes three months each way.

Seals migrate as well, but those that breed in temperate places do not travel very far. Monk seals and gray seals wander away from their breeding beaches to molt, and to feed for a few months. Southern elephant seals, on the other hand, breed on Antarctic islands and migrate as far as 2,000 km (1,240 mi) northward to feed in winter. Sometimes the seals reach western Australia.

The walrus is rather unusual. Its pups are born in May on an ice floe and they stay with their mother for as long as three years, occasionally moving to a nearby floe. The ice drifts with the changing currents, and the walruses are carried on a circular route that may be as much as 1,000 km (620 mi).

A scene from the Falkland Islands in the South Atlantic Ocean, where the Antarctic fur seal (left) and the southern elephant seal (right) migrate to breed.

Fuel for the journey

Some animals must migrate in order to find food, and others must find food in order to migrate. In the first group, wildebeest and caribou travel from place to place in search of fresh grass, feeding as they go. Kob antelope in the Sudan are different – on their journey south they must cross a dry area where there is no grass to eat. To survive, they must have fed well before leaving the good grass of the north.

Long-distance seabird migrants, including the Arctic tern, can feed wherever they are. However, the polar waters where they spend the summer are much richer in food than the sea near the equator, which they must cross twice a year.

Salmon stop feeding when they return to fresh water. They must be fat and healthy when they leave the sea, especially if they are to return to it again after breeding.

Land birds such as thrushes or swallows must fatten themselves up before they cross deserts or make long sea crossings. Geese are water birds, but they cannot feed out at sea, so they too must fatten up before they leave the land.

Each spring several species of hummingbirds fly across the Gulf of Mexico to nest in western parts of the United States. They return to South America in the autumn. Scientists have found that the tiny birds cannot store enough fat to make the 3,000-km (1,860 mi) trip. The birds solve the problem by flying very high, where there are air currents that help to speed them on their way.

Scientists are learning more and more, but some of the wonders of migration may never be explained. One important lesson is that migratory animals need protection in all the countries along the route of their amazing journeys.

Opposite *The black-chinned hummingbird (top left), ruby-throated hummingbird (top right) and rufous hummingbird (below) all migrate from South America to the western United States. They are shown feeding on hibiscus flowers.*

Glossary

Arctic Circle An imaginary circle around the world that passes through Alaska, Canada, Greenland, Norway, Finland and Russia. It divides the frozen north from the warmer south.

Artificial Unnatural or man-made.

Bedouin Nomadic Arab peoples who live in the deserts of Arabia, Jordan and Syria and in the Sahara.

Compass An instrument for finding direction with a needle that always points to magnetic north.

Estuary The wide part of a river where it flows into the sea.

Floe A floating piece of flat ice.

Hibernate To sleep through the winter.

Krill Small shrimp-like creatures of the oceans.

Lapland The name for the area north of the Arctic Circle that includes parts of Norway, Sweden, Finland and Russia.

Magnetic Field The field of force around a magnet and around the earth.

Molt To shed old hairs or feathers, and grow new ones.

Navigate To find one's way.

Nomadic Wandering, with no fixed home.

Northern Hemisphere The northern half of the earth.

Oasis (pl. oases) A watering place in a desert.

Planetarium A building that recreates the movement of the sun, moon and stars. These are imitated by shining lights onto a domed ceiling.

Plankton The many different tiny animals and plants that spend all or part of their lives drifting near the surface of the sea.

Predator An animal that kills other animals for food.

Pupate To change from a caterpillar to a pupa (chrysalis), which will split to produce an adult.

Roost To find a safe place to sleep. The word is usually used of birds, but also of some insects, such as mosquitoes.

Southern Hemisphere The southern half of the earth.

Temperate Moderate. The parts of the earth between the polar and tropical regions are called the temperate zones.

Transparent Clear, see-through.

Tundra The grasslands beyond the northernmost trees in the Arctic.

Picture Acknowledgments

The publishers would like to thank those who provided photographs for this book:
Bryan and Cherry Alexander 17; Bruce Coleman Limited 20 (Jeff Foott); Survival Anglia Limited 9 and 27 (Jeff Foott), 22 (Cindy Buxton/Annie Price).

Further information

You can find out more about migration by reading the following books:

All About Migration by John Sanders. Troll Associates, 1984.

Amazing Facts about Animals by Gyles Brandreth. Doubleday, 1981.

Animal Territories by Daniel Cohen. Hastings, 1975.

Animals that Migrate by Caroline Arnold. Carolrhoda, 1982.

Animals that Travel by Gwynne Vevers. Merrimack, 1981.

The Answer Book about Animals by Mary Elting. Putnam Publishers, 1984.

How Animals Behave by Donald J. Crump, ed. National Geographic Society, 1984.

How Animals Live by Philip Steele. Franklin Watts, 1985.

Misplaced Animals, Plants, and Other Living Creatures by Alice Hopf. McGraw, 1975.

Mysteries of Migration by Robert M. McClung. Garrard, 1983.

Some of the wildlife programs that are shown on television follow animals on their migrations. You may find that some birds regularly fly to a breeding ground in your state, or that other birds fly over your local area while on their way elsewhere. You might also like to join an organization that helps to protect wild animals from extinction. Some useful addresses are:

Audubon Naturalist Society of the Central Atlantic States
8940 Jones Mill Road
Chevy Chase, Maryland 20815
301–652–9188

The Conservation Foundation
1717 Massachusetts Avenue, N.W.
Washington, D.C. 20036
202–797–4300

Greenpeace USA
1611 Connecticut Avenue, N.W.
Washington, D.C. 20009
202–462–1177

The Humane Society of the USA
2100 L Street, N.W.
Washington, D.C. 20037
202–452–1100

The International Fund for Animal Welfare
P.O. Box 193
Yarmouth Port, Massachusetts 02675
617–362–4944

National Wildlife Federation
1412 16th Street, N.W.
Washington, D.C. 20036
202–797–6800

World Wildlife Fund
1255 23rd Street, N.W.
Washington, D.C. 20037
202–293–4800

Index

591.525 Penny, Malcolm.
PEN
         Animal migration.

                                    012341
$8.99

DATE			

√

© THE BAKER & TAYLOR CO.